Stuffed

Stuffed

Eric Walters

orca soundings

ORCA BOOK PUBLISHERS

Library and Archives Canada Cataloguing in Publication

Walters, Eric, 1957-
Stuffed / Eric Walters.

(Orca soundings)
ISBN 978-1-55143-519-0 (bound) ISBN 978-1-55143-500-8 (pbk.)

I. Title. II. Series.

PS8595.A598S88 2006   jC813'.54   C2006-900400-5

Summary: Ian decides to take a stand against a fast-food multinational.

First published in the United States, 2006
Library of Congress Control Number: 2006921004

Orca Book Publishers gratefully acknowledges the support for its publishing
programs provided by the following agencies: the Government of Canada
through the Book Publishing Industry Development Program and the
Canada Council for the Arts, and the Province of British Columbia through
the BC Arts Council and the Book Publishing Tax Credit.

Cover design by Teresa Bubela
Cover photography by Getty Images

Orca Book Publishers   Orca Book Publishers
PO Box 5626 Stn.B   PO Box 468
Victoria, BC Canada   Custer, WA USA
V8R 6S4   98240-0468

www.orcabook.com
Printed and bound in Canada.
Printed on 100% PCW recycled paper.

11 10 09 • 6 5 4

For those who make
healthy choices in life.

Chapter One

The credits started rolling up the screen. Behind the credits were pictures of people—overwhelmingly overweight people with rolls of fat bulging over jeans and busting out of tops, with triple chins, and wearing clothes big enough to be circus tents.

The lights came on and Mrs. Fletcher walked to the front of the classroom, turned off the DVD and clicked off the TV.

"That was quite an interesting documentary," she said.

It was called *Stuffed*, and it was all about Frankie's, the gigantic fast-food chain. It was all about how their food was filled with fat and chemicals and how eating it could make people overweight, unhealthy, sick and could basically kill them.

"Comments?" Mrs. Fletcher asked.

"That was disgusting," Julia snapped. Julia was one of my best friends. "Just disgusting!"

"It was pretty gross," Oswald agreed. He was my *best* friend.

Two weeks ago he might have agreed or he might have disagreed with Julia. Now he did nothing but agree with anything and everything she said. Two weeks ago he and Julia had stopped being friends and started being boyfriend and girlfriend.

"It made me hungry," Trevor said. A chorus of laughter followed his words.

"Hungry?" Julia demanded, sounding not only surprised but offended. "How could you possibly even think about eating after what we just saw?"

"I like Frankie's food," Trevor said. "It's tasty and big...really big...and I like big food."

Trevor looked like he could have been *in* the documentary.

Julia opened her mouth to answer, but Mrs. Fletcher cut her off. "What do other people think?" she asked.

I thought that was pretty smart on her part—cutting Julia off before she said something about Trevor that we were all probably thinking but nobody should have said.

Other people joined into the debate. It was creating a lot of opinions—but then again, it was a pretty strong documentary.

The film was about some guy who lived on nothing but Frankie's food. Breakfast, lunch and dinner, he ate nothing but Frankie's. Sausages and coffee and hotcakes and hash browns for breakfast; burgers and fries and onion rings and Coke and root beer for lunch and dinner. Every day, every meal for sixty days. By the end he was fat and sluggish and depressed.

"What was the most interesting thing you learned?" Mrs. Fletcher asked the class.

"That they put sugar in everything, including the French fries and onion rings," a girl said.

"I couldn't believe the amount of sugar that guy had eaten," another boy said. "It was like a small mountain!"

There had been a scene in the movie where sugar—equal to all the sugar he'd eaten—was piled on a table. The amount of sugar was so massive it slipped off the edges of the table.

"What grossed me out the most was all that fat!" Julia said.

"That was sick!" Oswald agreed. "And I don't mean that in a good way."

After the sugar scene they had glass jars filled with greasy, slimy fat—equal to the amount he'd eaten during the two months.

"Those were both wonderful visual displays. How many people are now less likely to eat at Frankie's?" Mrs. Fletcher asked.

Three-quarters of the class put up their hands.

"Those who didn't raise their hands, could you explain why it didn't affect you in the same way?"

"Frankie's food tastes the best," a boy said.

"Yeah," Trevor agreed, "especially the triple bacon cheeseburger melt." Trevor's eyes were closed as if he was picturing the burger in his mind. I wouldn't have been surprised if a string of drool had come out of his mouth.

That was actually my favorite burger too—I liked it, but I thought Trevor was *in love* with it.

"And you still would eat one of those after watching the film?" Julia questioned.

"Why not?" Trevor asked.

"Did you fall asleep during the movie?" Julia demanded.

"Julia," Mrs. Fletcher cautioned.

"But Mrs. Fletcher, that's the very worst thing on the whole menu!" Julia protested. "Each one has over twelve hundred calories and more fat than anybody should eat in an entire day!

That guy gained thirty-seven pounds because of that burger!"

"It wasn't just the burgers," Trevor said. "And besides, it's not like I'm going to eat there every day."

"Trevor has a point," Mrs. Fletcher said. "Now, this documentary focused on just one fast-food chain, but what about the others?"

"They're all the same," Julia said.

"Are they?" Mrs. Fletcher asked.

"Sure they are. They all serve fried, fatty, sugary foods."

"Yes they do, but don't most chains offer healthy alternatives?" Mrs. Fletcher questioned.

"Well…"

"Can't you get salads and fruit platters and yogurt, mineral water and juices at most of the other places?"

"I guess so," Julia said.

"So at most fast-food restaurants it is possible to eat healthier, if not healthy."

"But not at Frankie's," Oswald said. "They don't have any of those things. It's like they're proud of being unhealthy."

"Their commercials do brag about offering the biggest servings of fries, the largest soft drinks and the most gigantic burgers," another person added.

"Ian," Mrs. Fletcher said, and I startled in my seat. "What do you think about all of this?"

"Me?"

"You. You've been very quiet through this whole discussion."

"Maybe I've learned that it's sometimes better to keep your mouth shut," I said.

"Sometimes it *is* better. But not in *my* class. And it's good to have you back in class," she said.

"It's nice to be back."

This was my first morning in class after a two-day suspension—I still couldn't believe that I'd been suspended!

Disrespectful conduct is what it said on the papers. What that meant is that I had an argument with my law teacher, Mr. Phillips. I'd made the terrible mistake of pointing out to him that he had no idea what he was talking about, that he was an idiot.

The jerk thought that because he was a law teacher he knew about the law. Both my parents were lawyers. My older sister and both my older brothers were lawyers. In my house we talked about the law. My parents had hoped I'd be a lawyer too. I wasn't sure what I was going to be, but I was pretty sure what I wasn't going to be—I wasn't going to be a lawyer, and I wasn't going to be a law teacher.

In the end, even after I was suspended, the school agreed that I'd been right and Phillips had been wrong. Unfortunately, both my school and my parents agreed that I probably shouldn't have sworn at him and told him he was an idiot—

even if he was. My father had said that if I hadn't sworn at him they would have fought the suspension.

"So, Ian, what did you think about *Stuffed*?" Mrs. Fletcher asked.

"I liked it. I mean, it made some good points. There were things he explained that I hadn't known. I'm not going to be eating at Frankie's…as often."

"As often?" Julia demanded. "Don't you mean ever again?"

"Ever again is a long time. Besides, I like the triple bacon cheeseburger melt too."

Julia shot me a disgusted look.

"I will never eat at a Frankie's again," Julia pronounced. "Never, not ever."

"How many people feel like Julia?" Mrs. Fletcher asked.

This time only five hands shot into the air. I noticed that Oswald's hand didn't go up. Lucky for him, Julia didn't notice.

"So the majority of you feel you will eat at Frankie's less often, but only a few of you think you will never eat there again," Mrs. Fletcher said.

"Too bad it isn't more people," Trevor said, and everybody looked at him in surprise. "Yeah, the less people that eat there, the shorter the lineups for those of us who do."

There was more laughter. As Mrs. Fletcher tried to settle down the students, the bell rang to signal the end of class.

"You're all dismissed!" Mrs. Fletcher yelled out. "And please, enjoy your lunch!"

Chapter Two

I settled into my seat at our table in the cafeteria and started pulling stuff out of my lunch bag. A peanut-butter-and-jelly sandwich on whole wheat, an apple, a couple of cookies and a Coke. Not bad. At least nothing fried or fatty.

Julia put down her lunch bag. I knew what would be inside—salad, either a chicken or tuna sandwich and a bottle of water. She hardly ever ate anything that wasn't healthy, so her threat not to eat at Frankie's again wasn't really going to cost them a lot of money.

"Where's Oswald?" she asked.

I shrugged. "He doesn't check his every move with *me*."

"What does that mean?" Julia asked.

"Nothing."

Nothing I was going to talk about, but I was getting mighty sick of him sucking up to her—agreeing with whatever she said, complimenting her, pretending he was actually interested in what she was saying. Man, it was ugly when friends became more than just friends. Oswald was being a chicken and Julia hadn't even noticed. At least she was pretending she hadn't noticed.

"I still can't get over you saying you'd still eat at Frankie's," Julia said.

"Everything in moderation," I said. "Socrates."

"Socrates would have been smart enough not to eat at Frankie's."

"I don't know," I said. "Didn't he die when he drank poison?"

"Frankie's is poison," Julia said. "I don't know why you can't see that."

Looking beyond Julia I caught sight of Oswald. He was carrying a tray. On the tray—there in plain view—was a Coke, a burger and a side order of fries. I started to smile.

"You think this is funny?" Julia questioned.

"Nope, nothing funny here. You just can't expect us all to be as convinced as you and Oswald."

"Convinced of what?" Oswald said as he put his tray down and took a seat.

"Convinced that…" Julia stopped talking, and her eyes got wide in disbelief as she stared at Oswald's lunch. "You bought French fries?"

"And a burger, and I do believe that is an order of onion rings...I think onions are a vegetable...aren't they?" I chided.

"How...how could you?" Julia demanded, sounding like Oswald had kicked a puppy or cheated on her.

He looked genuinely confused. "I didn't do anything. I was just getting my lunch and—" He suddenly got it. "But I didn't get this from Frankie's."

"It doesn't matter where you got it from. It's still all poison!"

"Don't forget about the onion rings," I said. "Onions are a—"

"Shut up, Ian!" Julia snapped. "You're not going to eat any of that are you?"

"I...I...I guess not...but I am hungry," Oswald replied.

"Wanna trade?" I asked.

"I spent five bucks on this meal," Oswald said.

"Then you should have spent your money on a fruit tray or a salad or a yogurt and some juice," Julia said. "You know they have all of those things in the cafeteria, right?"

"Sure, right, I know," Oswald said.

"So…you want to trade or just toss it?" I asked.

Oswald shook his head slowly and scowled. "We can trade."

He pushed the tray across the table and I slid my lunch back to him.

"You already took a bite," he said, holding up the sandwich.

"Sorry. I didn't know we'd be trading. You want some fries?" I asked, holding them out. They were still steamy hot and smelled good.

"No thanks."

"Don't say I didn't offer."

"I was telling Ian that I was never going to eat at Frankie's again," Julia said. "And I told him I wasn't the only one. You're not going to eat there anymore, right?" she asked Oswald.

"No, of course not."

I made a little motion like he was being whipped—which he was. Julia didn't notice, but Oswald did and looked embarrassed.

"But you will eat at those other fast-food places, right?" I asked, tightening the screws a little bit more on him.

"Maybe...sometimes...but only the healthy stuff...mostly," Oswald said.

"I'm surprised you aren't becoming a vegetarian, like Julia." I was really enjoying watching him squirm.

"I'm not eating as much meat," he said.

"Really? I'm only one step away from being a vegetarian myself," I said.

"You are?" Julia asked.

17

"I only eat animals that *are* vegetarians."

"Sometimes you are such a jerk!" Julia said.

"Sometimes? That's a serious step up from what you usually say. Besides, if you think about it I'm eating French-fried *potatoes*, *onion* rings, and I doubt there really is any meat in this hamburger either."

"Seriously," Julia said, "are you saying that movie had no effect on you?"

I took a big bite from the burger and chewed it slowly, swallowing before I answered.

"I think it was pretty powerful, and I really can understand why somebody would choose to not ever eat there again, or not as often. Really, I don't think I'm going to be going there for a long time myself."

Julia gave a smug, satisfied little smile.

"I wonder how Frankie's feels about the film," Oswald said.

"Not happy would be my guess. Really, really not happy," Julia said.

I shook my head. "I don't think they could care less."

"How can you say that?" Julia asked.

"It's just some little documentary film that hardly anybody is going to see. Did either of you ever hear of it before today?"

They both shook their heads.

"It wasn't in the movie theaters, and I doubt you can even rent it at Blockbuster. Frankie's is a multinational, billion-dollar company with thousands of franchises. Do you really think it matters to them if a few people decide not to eat there so often?"

Julia didn't answer right away, which meant she knew I was right and didn't want to admit it.

"Well?" I asked, pushing her.

"I can't control what other people do or don't do," Julia said.

Other than Oswald, I thought, but didn't say it. I knew where the line was—even if I did choose to step over it every now and again. I grabbed a couple of French fries and stuffed them in my mouth. They really weren't as good as Frankie's fries.

Chapter Three

"Well, I think that pretty well settles it," my father said as he got up from the dining room table, taking his dishes with him.

"I'm glad you agree," my mother said. "And it's a sign of your increasing maturity that you're able to admit defeat."

"Defeat!" my father exclaimed, spinning around on his heels. "The only defeat here is yours! I very successfully defended my position and exposed the faults in your argument!"

"There are no faults in my argument. Perhaps the logic was too refined for you to understand," she said.

"Could you two stop it?" I said, cutting them both off before they could continue.

My father looked surprised by my outburst. "We're having a friendly debate."

"Yes, a healthy exchange of ideas," my mother added.

"No, you're not. You're holding a full trial. All you need is a judge and a jury to deliver a verdict."

"A judge," my father said. "That would be a good thing." He looked at my mother and then they both looked at me and smiled.

"I'm not being the judge," I said, figuring out what he had in mind.

"Why not?" my father asked. "We trust your judgment and you heard our arguments."

"I heard *some* of what you both said. I drifted off a couple of times."

"Even better," my father said.

"How can that be better?"

"Half the judges I've ever appeared before fell asleep on the bench."

"It doesn't matter. I'm not giving a verdict here. Couldn't we have the occasional supper conversation that didn't end up as a trial?"

My mother got up from the table and started to help my father clear the dishes. "I guess us having these discussions is an occupational hazard. If you had two parents who were doctors instead of lawyers, we'd be talking medicine."

"Actually, if we were both doctors you wouldn't even *be* here," my father said.

"He has a point, Ian."

My parents had met in a courtroom. He was the lawyer for one side and she was the lawyer for the other side. They started fighting there in the court, continued fighting afterward when they went for a friendly drink and didn't stop until they were married six months later. They went on to form a partnership—Cheevers and Cheevers. Now they were just about the best-known—and feared—trial lawyers in the city.

"Do you want to wash or dry?" my mother asked.

"I'll do whatever you want," my father answered.

She slipped her arm around his waist and gave him a kiss on the cheek. People who didn't know them and heard them arguing with each other would have thought they hated each other. They didn't. They were almost sick-eningly in love. Twenty-seven years of marriage and four kids later they still held hands and giggled at each other's bad jokes.

I got up and cleared my dishes away. "It would be nice to just have a normal family discussion over dinner sometimes," I said.

"What do you mean?" my father asked.

"You know, talking about what's on TV, or a movie, or what I did at school today."

"What *did* you do at school today?" my mother asked.

"Nothing."

"Thanks for sharing that," my father joked.

"We could just talk. Especially when we have someone over for dinner. It can be confusing for them."

"Julia never seems to mind," my father said. "I think she enjoys our discussions."

"Julia likes arguing even more than the two of you do," I said.

"She does enjoy a good discussion. That girl would make one fine lawyer."

That was just about the biggest compliment my father could ever give. My not wanting to follow in the family tradition bothered them, even if they didn't say much about it.

"Speaking of Julia, we haven't seen much of her lately. It's been weeks since she joined us for dinner," my mother said.

"I think she's at Oswald's tonight."

"Oswald's? We haven't seen as much of him lately either," my mother said. "It wasn't because of something we said, was it?"

I shook my head. "Actually it was something Oswald said to Julia. He said, 'Do you want to go to a movie, and do you want to be my girlfriend?'"

"Julia and Oswald are dating?" my mother questioned.

"I guess that's the word."

"How long has this been going on?"

"Officially about two weeks," I said, although I wanted to say "way too long."

"Funny, I can't picture the two of them together," my father said.

"Me neither," my mother agreed.

I could see their point. I'd actually seen the two of them together and still couldn't picture it.

"I always thought Julia would end up with you," my mother said.

"Me?" I exclaimed.

"Yeah, I thought the same thing," my father agreed.

"But Julia and I do nothing but fight!" I argued.

"Sounds like your mother and me," my father said with a chuckle.

"I had visions of someday changing the name of the firm from Cheevers and Cheevers to Cheevers and Cheevers and Cheevers and Cheevers and Cheevers."

I shook my head. "Could we just go back to arguing legal issues?"

They both laughed.

"Nothing wrong with a little healthy debate," my father said.

"Tell that to Mr. Phillips," I muttered.

"Healthy debate stopped when you swore at him," my mother said firmly.

"If either of us had said to a judge what you said to your teacher, we'd be jailed for contempt of court," my father said.

"What would you have said to a judge who was so clearly wrong?" I asked.

"I'd politely point out his error," my father answered.

"And if he didn't listen?"

"Well…"

"He wouldn't have sworn at the judge," my mother said. "Your father would have appealed the judge's error."

"That was my problem. Nobody to appeal to."

"Your principal explained that you could have spoken to her to try to correct the situation," my father said.

"My principal is a bigger idiot than Phillips!"

"This discussion is getting us nowhere. How about since I'm washing and your father is drying that you put things away?"

"How about if I finish my homework first?"

"I guess that makes sense. The witness is excused."

Chapter Four

I went downstairs to my room. I'd recently changed rooms—from upstairs, where all the other bedrooms were, to a room in the basement that used to be a guest bedroom. I opened the door a few inches. It wouldn't open much more than that because of all the stuff on the floor. I squeezed through the gap and then closed the door tightly after me.

Every piece of clothing I owned was spread out across the floor. The only exceptions were a suit I wore for weddings and funerals, which was hanging in the closet, and a laundry basket that had some newly washed, clean clothes. The basket sat at the end of my bed.

To the uninformed observer it would have looked like my room was in complete chaos, as if it had been ransacked and robbed, or a small indoor tornado had swept through. Neither of those was true. There was a system in place. Sweaters, hoodies and long-sleeved shirts were in the far left corner, by the window. T-shirts were in the far right-hand corner. Pants and shorts were in the near corner, by the closet, and socks and underwear occupied the final corner. The four clothing groups then spread out from their respective resting places and met, sort of merging, in the very center of the room. That's where I stood when I was getting dressed. Everything was within my reach. It was, as I said, a system.

My mother had other words for it, but we had a deal. It was my room and I could keep it any way I wanted as long as she didn't have to look at it. That was why the door was closed all the time. Actually I wouldn't have minded the door being open to allow cross-ventilation with the window. The place could use an airing out.

I knew my mother knew the condition of my room. And she knew I knew she knew, but she still hadn't said a word—at least not yet. It was sort of like a game we were playing. Correction, it was more like a game *I* was playing and she was involuntarily part of.

I sat down at my desk and shifted some dishes around so I had a place to spread out my books. I had a computer science assignment due the next week. I was almost finished. Technically, when I told my parents I had homework to do, I really didn't have anything I needed to do right now. They were always good about letting me off chore duty if I had schoolwork to do. There was always something I could do, or pretend to do, to get out of doing dishes.

Actually, if I continued to accumulate dishes in my room, soon there wouldn't be dishes in the kitchen to wash. At last count I had twenty-seven different plates, bowls, cups and mugs spread around the room. Each contained different types and quantities of food and drink. Some of them had been around long enough to develop into interesting little science experiments. I was fascinated by the variety of colors and shapes of mold and fungi that could be created. I considered this to be my version of low-maintenance indoor gardening. Some people grew roses. I grew things that might eventually develop into a new antibiotic. The only downside was that a couple were starting to send out a real smell. Certainly not roses. Maybe I should consider taking some of them upstairs the next time I went.

That would make my mother happy. The other night she'd asked my dad—when I was within earshot—if he knew where all the dishes "*were disappearing to.*" He said he had "*no idea.*" Give me a break; we all knew they were hiding in my room.

I grabbed the converter and clicked on my TV. I raced through the channels, looking for what I wanted. There it was—channel 47—*The Simpsons*. Instantly I recognized the episode, but then again, I recognized all the episodes because I'd seen them all at least a dozen times. With all the new specialty channels available, I was waiting to subscribe to *The Simpsons Network*.

In some ways I practically had that. If you searched through all the channels, there seemed to be a *Simpsons* episode somewhere almost all the time.

I grabbed a second remote—the one for my stereo—and it came to life. I clicked on a CD and the music started with a loud thud, startling me. I adjusted the sound. It couldn't be too loud or I couldn't hear *The Simpsons* at the same time. Somehow the rap lyrics—one of my favorites from Sage Francis—worked well with the scenes on the screen. It almost seemed like Bart was listening to the music as he sat in his bedroom with his broken leg, looking through his telescope. I looked up at my window. The curtains were open and I had the bizarre thought that maybe Bart was listening to Sage Francis while looking in my window.

I wiggled the mouse and the computer screen came to life. I opened up the file where I was writing my computer science assignment. Next I opened up the textbook to the right place. I was almost finished. All I needed to do was write one more point and then do the conclusion. Of course "almost finished" and "happily finished" were different. The project was about the use of e-mail for mass communication. I had all the technical stuff, the textbook stuff, but it was dry and boring. I needed to liven it up, but I didn't know how.

My fingers sat on the keys, but nothing seemed to be flowing into them. I couldn't think of what to write. I didn't seem to be able to focus. Then I realized what was missing.

I ran the pointer down to the bottom of the screen and double-clicked on the MSN icon. The screen opened up to reveal my Hotmail address and a second line for

my password. I typed it in. S…h…a…
d…o…w. Shadow, the name of my dog.
I'd read somewhere that kids, pets and
birthdays were the first three things a
hacker tried when he was figuring out
how to break into your account. I figured
if anybody was desperate enough to
want to hack into my mail, I wouldn't
make it too difficult—obviously he had
enough problems.

I hit enter and the screen filled
with my whole contact list. I scrolled
down, looking to see who was online.
There was Oswald—*The Wizzzzard of
Ozzie*—and Julia was online too—*The
Royal Jewels*.

I clicked onto Oswald first.

hey Oz—how r u? I typed in.
good. u? he replied.
ok. what are u doing? I asked.
nmjc. His shorthand, which meant
"nothing much, just chilling."

wanna go n get something to eat
l8ter? I asked.
go where? he asked.
frankie's ☺
you're cruel, he answered back.
may b cruel, but not whipped!
wanna see if J wants to go with
us?
not funny. g2g, he typed.
got to go where? I asked.
Supper. Not frankie's. Brb after
finish.

I clicked on Julia's name and her
window opened up. Beside her name
was a picture of a cartoon greyhound.
Julia was trying to convince her parents
to adopt a former racing greyhound to
go along with their two poodles.

I told her there was a fine line between
being a person who owned dogs and
somebody who was a dog person, living
alone, never getting married, wearing

fuzzy slippers around the neighborhood and talking to themselves. That line was the third dog.

> hey, j, wat?
> Her answer came right away:
> nm—u?
> homewrk. still thinking bout frankie's? I typed in.
> just came out of a chat rm—lots of ppl think frankie's sucks big time—think bout not eating their crap.
> don't blame em—I never eat anybdy's crap—leaves a bad taste in mouth.
> LoL

Laugh out loud. That made me smile. I was glad she found that funny. Julia and Oswald had both taken a curious dip into the serious pool since they'd started dating.

know wat bugs me most bout
frankie's? I asked.
trying to poison u? Julia replied.
trix they play, I answered.
don't understand
stupid plastic toys, games, play
place—all to get u to eat there—
tricking little kids, I explained.
get it. sort of like giving kids
candy cigarettes so they become
smokers.
x-actly! these ppl running the
company live in big houses with
fancy cars cause they trix stupid
ppl into eating at frankie's. don't
like to be trixed
u'd rather be poisoned than
tricked, Julia wrote.
Yeah. Your point?
I'd like ppl to know they do both
n not eat there anymore
What can you do? I asked.
not much. talk w friends. tell em

not to eat ther. told 5 ppl tonight
on msn.
any of em listen? I typed in.
3 of em g2g c ya l8ter.
c ya l8ter.

Her screen closed and I was back to
my contact list. I scrolled down. There
were one hundred and eighteen people
on my list. I looked at the ones who
were online right now. There were eight
people from school. A couple from
my basketball team. My cousin Sean,
who lived on the East Coast. There
was Barbie, who went under the MSN
name *foxxxxy lady*. She said she lived
in California, was my age and claimed
she was really hot. I didn't know if
any of those things were true, but I did
like talking to her. I wasn't even sure
how I originally connected to her, but
contact lists could be strange like that.
You could have people from around the

corner or around the world. It was just bizarre how we all were connected.

Then it hit me. An idea so strange that it just might work.

Chapter Five

I sat down at the cafeteria table right across from Julia and Oswald. They were holding hands under the table. Cute. No, correct that—stupid. Oswald was struggling to open his milk with just his left hand. Did he think if he let go she'd float away?

"Here," I said as I reached over and ripped the carton open.

"Thanks," he mumbled.

"Let me know if your shoelaces come undone. It's even harder to tie them with one hand."

Oswald looked embarrassed but held tight to Julia. Julia just ignored my comment.

"I've been thinking a lot about Frankie's," I said.

"Probably drooling," Julia said.

"Maybe a little bit," I admitted.

"I don't know how you can even think about eating there," she said, sounding suitably disgusted.

"To tell you the truth I was thinking about how to have people not eat at Frankie's."

"You were?" Julia leaned forward across the table.

I nodded. "I have an idea."

"You do? What's your idea?"

"Before I tell you I have to give you some background."

"Okay, shoot."

"To begin with, it's not realistic to expect people to never, ever eat at Frankie's again," I said.

"I don't see why not!" Julia argued.

"There are lots of reasons. Sometimes there's no other place to eat, or that's the place where your father wants to go to eat, or maybe because, let's face it, some of their food just tastes good."

"If poison tasted good would you eat it?" Julia questioned.

"Probably only once," I admitted. "But lots of people like Frankie's. They probably have the best fries around. Even Oswald would agree with that," I said, gesturing to him.

His eyes widened and his mouth dropped open. I didn't know if he was feeling afraid or confused. Maybe he was confused about why he was so afraid of Julia.

"Come on, Oswald, just answer the question…honestly."

"Well…they have pretty good fries."

Julia shot him a look and then folded her arms across her chest. Obviously she'd let go of his hand. Maybe that's what he was afraid of.

"So," I said, cutting through the tension, "what is realistic is to ask people to eat less at Frankie's or to make Frankie's change the food they serve."

"Not eating there at all is eating there less," Julia maintained.

"But not realistic. I'm suggesting we pick a day, one day, and we don't eat there."

"That's your idea?" Julia asked in disbelief. "That for *one* day we don't eat at Frankie's?"

"That's part of my idea."

"Then it's a pretty *stupid* idea! There are lots of days when people don't eat there. That guy in the documentary is the only person in the world who ate at Frankie's every day."

"My plan isn't stupid. Just shut up for a minute and listen. I'm not talking about you and Oswald and me not eating at Frankie's. I'm talking about *everybody*."

Julia snorted. It was quite the feminine-sounding noise—if the female was a pig.

"So should I just climb up on the table and yell out an order that everybody is forbidden to eat at Frankie's next Tuesday?" Julia taunted.

"Let me see…um…wrong…wrong and, yes, wrong again." I paused for dramatic effect. "First, it isn't going to be an order, but an invitation. Second, Tuesday is too soon. I was thinking the Friday after this Friday. And third, I'm not talking about everybody here," I said, motioning around the cafeteria. "I'm talking about every*body*, every*where*."

"What does that mean?" Oswald asked.

"It means all people...here...there... everywhere."

"Yeah, like we know everybody," Julia said.

"You don't, but you do know some-body who knows somebody who knows somebody else who knows every other person on the *entire* planet."

Julia looked confused. Oswald looked even more confused than usual.

"Look, you know that project I'm working on for computer science," I said.

"It's about the Internet, right?" Oswald said.

"It's about how the Internet can be used to spread a message," I explained.

"And you think if we sent out a couple of messages, we can talk our friends into not eating at Frankie's?" Julia asked. "I already talked to nine or ten people on MSN last night about Frankie's being poison."

"I'm talking the Internet, and I'm talking MSN, but I'm not talking about just a few people," I said. "How many people do you have on your contact list?" I asked Julia.

"I don't know exactly, but maybe a hundred and forty or a hundred and fifty."

"And you, Oswald?"

"Eighty or ninety."

"I'm about the same. Now, what if we all put out a mass e-mail, a blast, to everybody on our contact lists. In that blast we have a message saying why Frankie's food is bad and asking them to stay away from Frankie's on that Friday."

"Two Fridays from now, right?" Oswald said.

"It doesn't have to be then, but I thought the timing was about right. We can call it Frankie's Free Friday."

"That's catchy," Oswald said.

"That was why I chose a Friday. There's something about the sound of all those f's."

"Okay, so I send out a blast to 140 people and you two send out another 90 messages each...so what?" Julia asked. "That's like 320 people...actually less because we have a lot of the same people on our contact lists, so some people would get three messages, one from each of us."

"We do have a lot of people in common," I agreed. "I'm thinking maybe only forty people on each of our lists would be different from the others'."

"So you think 120 people are going to make a difference?" Julia asked.

"No, I was thinking less than that. Probably half of those people will just delete the message and put it in their trash."

"So it's a waste of time," Julia said.

"No, it's a *start*. What if those 60 people who do respond send out a blast to everybody on *their* contact list? That would mean 60 people with 40 contacts each is 2,400 people. And then if half of those people do a blast of 40 people, there would be 48,000 contacts who receive the message."

"That can't be right," Oswald said.

"Yes, it is. Look." I pulled a piece of paper out of my pocket and unfolded it. "See for yourself."

Oswald and Julia looked at my figures.

"And you see that by the sixth generation—the sixth time it spreads out— the message could reach three hundred and eighty-four *million* people."

Julia looked up at me. "This actually could work, couldn't it?"

"If the message goes out to that many people and only some of them listen, you can make a difference in how many people eat at Frankie's. We actually could make it a Frankie's Free Friday." I paused. "So?"

"So, I think we should do it," Julia said.

"Oswald?" I asked, although I knew Julia had already given *his* answer.

"I'm in. What do we do now?" he asked.

"Let me draft the letter, and then I'll MSN you both tonight and we can go for it."

"Tonight?" Julia asked, sounding surprisingly hesitant.

"No point in waiting. The sooner we start, the sooner we finish."

"It's just that Oswald and I were going out," Julia said.

"Hopefully you won't be going out all night."

Chapter Six

I sat down at the computer. I needed to write the letter we were going to send out. I knew what I wanted to say— sort of, but not exactly. This had to be perfect. The success, or failure, of this whole project depended on what I wrote. I had been thinking about it a lot, and I knew what I wanted to write. I just had to write it.

Here it goes.

Hello Friend,

This is not a junk letter and I'm not trying to sell you something. I don't want your money.

I want to tell you about something and invite you to take part in something big.

You all know Frankie's. You've all eaten there. What you might not know is that Frankie's is maybe the worst place you could eat. Worse than all the other fast-food places because it's the only one that doesn't serve any healthy food at all! My class watched a documentary called "Stuffed," and we learned that Frankie's food makes you fat and unhealthy and even sick. The people who run Frankie's give away toys and trinkets and run contests to get us to eat there.

It feels like they're tricking us to get us to eat their food.

My friends and I are tired of Frankie's taking advantage of us. We're proposing a boycott. We're calling it "Frankie's Free Friday"—a day when nobody eats at Frankie's! We're proposing that we do this on Friday, April 13. We want to make Friday the 13th unlucky for Frankie's.

And, we need your help to make it happen. Here's how it works. We're blasting this message out to 40 people on our contact lists. We want you to forward this message to 40 people on your list and ask them to send it out to 40 people on their list, and so on and so on. If we all do this, we can reach millions and millions of people and we can make a difference. We can say

to Frankie's, "We're not being
fooled any longer...give us some
real food to eat!"

I read through the letter. It said what
I wanted to say and, according to my
spell-checker, everything was even
spelled right. I knew Julia wouldn't be
completely happy. She'd want me to use
stronger words—maybe call the food
poison or something like that, but I had
decided against it. If she didn't like it,
she should have written it.

I copied the message and then clicked
on the MSN icon at the bottom of the
page. My contact list came up. I clicked
on both Oswald and Julia and worked
my way through the list, deciding which
forty people were going to get my
message. I tried to aim for people who
I figured wouldn't be on either of their
lists, people who were far away. I wanted
this message to go across the country.

There it was, forty contacts all ready to get the same message. This was the first step. All I had to do was send it. My finger hovered above the Enter key. Once I pushed that button, the message would be gone and I couldn't get it back. It would shoot off in forty different directions to forty different people. Some of them were just around the corner, and most were within the city, but a few were going to cross the entire country. Instantly.

It might mean nothing. It might mean a lot. I pushed *Send*. I saw the little icon—*sending mail*. It flashed, flashed, flashed—bang—it was gone. Now all I had to do was wait and see what was going to happen.

Another message window made a warbling sound as it popped up on the bottom of my screen. I was having trouble finishing my paper on "The Power of the Internet for Mass Communication" because people on the Internet kept trying to communicate with me.

I clicked on it and the message opened up on the screen. It was my friend Barbie in California. How cool was that—her name was Barbie, she claimed she had blond hair and she lived in California. Too bad she didn't live in Malibu, 'cause that would have been perfect...well, perfect if my display name had been Ken instead of I-Man.

> hey, I-man, how's it going?
> good. u get my message about frankie's? I typed.
> got and sent. 40 ppl.
> thx for doing.
> any word on other ppl doing it? she asked.
> u are # 6 that I herd from.

do u think this will work? Barbie
asked.
hope so. g2g
l8ter

It was unbelievable. In only an hour,
six of the people I'd blasted had popped
up. Including Barbie, that made three
who had instantly sent out a blast to
people on their contact lists. I chatted
with the other three who had responded,
and they all agreed to do the same thing.
That meant my one message had now
gone out to at least two hundred and
eighty people—all within one hour!

I scanned my contact list. Neither
Oswald nor Julia was online. They were
probably still out together doing something. Together. Without me. Now that
they were a couple, they did things as a
pair. Before, three of us had seemed like
the right number. I missed that. I missed
them. Now I was a third wheel. No point

in crying about it. I was smart enough to know the two of them wouldn't last forever. I was actually surprised it had lasted this long. The problem was that when this strange couple thing was over, we'd still never be able to get back what we had. That was over.

Chapter Seven

"Ian!"

I turned around. It was Julia, running through the hall, barging by and through people.

"Hey," I said, trying to sound casual.

"Did you check your MSN this morning?" she asked.

"I didn't need to check. I was on it until almost three in the morning."

"Then you know how incredibly fast things are moving. Do you know *I* got your message—from *three* different people—people who had received your message and then passed it on, and I was one of the people they passed it on to!"

"Actually," I said and smiled, "somebody already sent the message back to me."

"You're kidding!"

I shook my head. "I tracked it back. Somebody on my blast list sent it to somebody else, who then sent it to me. They didn't notice my e-mail address on the bottom as the guy who had started the chain."

"That's amazing. One of those people who sent me the message is my cousin in Boston. Nobody I know would even know him, but somehow it got to him and then back to me. Unbelievable!" Julia shrieked.

"The power of the Internet...like I said."

"Not that I doubted you, but this is wild."

I fought the urge to say something about how I really did think that she doubted me. I kept my mouth shut.

"It's funny, but I was going to include my cousin on my blast so we could reach far away," Julia said.

"What movie did you and Oswald see?" I asked.

"It was very good. At least *I* thought it was very good."

"But Oswald didn't?"

"He has the worst taste in movies of anybody I've ever met."

"Just because somebody doesn't like the same thing as you doesn't mean they have bad taste. He can have his own opinion."

"I know he can have his own opinion. I just wish he wouldn't tell me what it was during the movie."

"I don't understand," I said.

"You know how Oswald likes to talk in the movies…make little comments? Well, I told him it was juvenile and he shouldn't do that anymore," she explained. "And somehow that led to us having an argument."

"It did?" I was shocked. Oswald was so whipped I didn't think he'd object to anything Julia said.

"Yes. He started sulking and then he wouldn't talk to me even *after* the movie ended and then I had to call him to try and talk things over. Eventually he apologized."

"*He* apologized?" I asked in disbelief.

"You know, for talking in the movies and then being difficult. Sometimes I just don't know about him." She paused. "About us."

"What don't you know?"

"I just think…maybe I shouldn't be talking to you about this because Oswald is your friend as well."

"And your friend too, before he became your boyfriend," I pointed out.

"It's just that you're the only other person I'm close to who I can tell what I'm thinking, who can maybe give me some advice."

"Not me," I said, holding up my hands. "I got nothing to say."

"You always have something to say," she argued.

"And I'm learning pretty quickly that sometimes the smartest thing a person can say is nothing. I gotta get to class now. See you, *and* Oswald, at lunch."

Chapter Eight

The whole day had been a blur. People—
some I knew, but most were just kids I'd
seen around the school—kept coming
up and telling me they'd received my
message. They'd heard through the
school grapevine that I was I-Man,
the guy who started it all.

They had got the e-mail from friends
and relatives and people they hardly

even knew. The message was sent by next-door neighbors or by people down the street, across the city and from the farthest reaches of the whole country. One guy told me he'd received his message from a friend in England... *England*! Somehow, in less than twelve hours, my message had crossed the Atlantic Ocean and bounced all the way back here. Talk about the potential for Internet mass communications!

I rushed into the house. I didn't even stop to grab something to eat. More than I was hungry, I was curious. I rushed downstairs, pushed through the door to my bedroom and plopped down at the computer. I wiggled the mouse and then clicked on my e-mail account. I wanted to see if I'd received any e-mails before I went online to check out the live messages on MSN.

The computer clicked over... *connecting...checking mail...receiving mail…receiving mail…receiving mail… receiving mail…receiving mail.*

Why was it taking so long to receive mail? I looked at the bottom to check the number of e-mails being down-loaded. The number was spinning…*127 messages…149…197…216…*

Now it felt like it was my head that was spinning. I pressed myself back in my chair, as if I needed to get a little more distance from the computer, and watched in awe and amazement as the number kept growing and growing and growing…*374 messages…410 messages…*This couldn't be real. This had to be a mistake, maybe a virus or something. It finally came to a stop.

678 unread messages.

Wow. I didn't know if I should be excited or scared or overwhelmed. Instead I felt all three. How in the world could you possibly get, and read, that many messages? Then I realized there was only one way. I clicked on the first message.

> I-Man. Good job. Frankie's sucks and we'll let them know that kids have the power to take em down. u rule!

Not a bad first message. I ruled. I clicked on the second message.

> I work at Frankie's. If you think the food is bad for you, you should see what goes on in the back room. Nobody spits in the food or anything. Spitting in the food would be better for you. Take it from me, nobody who works here eats here. Peace out.

That message was disturbing as well as reassuring. Next message.

Wat are u, some sort of veggie freak? y don't you stop hugging trees n be a man n eat real burgers. your e-mail shouldn't be I-Man it should be I-girl!

I wanted to answer that one, but I didn't have time. I still had—I looked at the screen—I still had *675 unread messages*. Then the computer chimed and started to download more mail. Bold-faced, unread messages flooded onto the screen. When I looked down again it read *697 unread messages*. In the time it had taken me to read three messages, another twenty had been sent. I had to read faster.

"Ian, time for dinner!" my father bellowed down the stairs.

"I don't have time!" I yelled back, my eyes glued on the screen, my fingers on the keys. I'd been working for close to three hours. I'd read over five hundred e-mails—and even answered forty or fifty.

The good news was almost all of them were telling me they agreed with what I was doing, and they were going to boycott Frankie's. A few people were angry and a few more were just crazy.

The bad news was another two hundred new messages had flooded in. Maybe I shouldn't think of it as bad news. It was good because it meant more people were planning to stay away from Frankie's.

There was a knock on my door and I turned around.

"Can I come in?" It was my father on the other side of the door.

"Sure…just come in carefully."

The door popped open a few inches before it jammed up against one of the piles on the floor. My father squeezed through the opening.

71

"You okay?" he asked.

"I'm fine."

"I thought it was strange that you weren't coming for dinner. Aren't you hungry?"

"Yeah, I guess I am. It's just that I don't have time to eat," I said.

"That doesn't look like schoolwork," he said, pointing at the e-mail screen.

"It is schoolwork…sort of. It's related to my project in computer science on mass communication through the Internet. I'm just answering my e-mails."

"How about if you eat first and then come back and do your e-mails later?" he said.

"I don't think I have time. This is important."

"How about if I bring a plate down here and you can eat while you work?" he suggested.

"That would be great."

"I'll get your mother to make it up and then *I'll* bring it down." He paused. "If your mother saw this place she'd lose her appetite and maybe her supper."

My father left and I went back to my e-mails. I clicked on another message.

> Dear Sir,
> It has come to our attention that you are pursuing a campaign to organize a boycott of our client, Frankie's Fast Food Restaurants. As legal counsel we are formally informing you that your actions may result in a lawsuit to recover damages, both in lost revenue and reputation. Furthermore—

I stopped reading, too stunned to go on. This wasn't possible…I was going to be sued by Frankie's!

Chapter Nine

"Okay, explain it to me again," my father said as he sat looking at the e-mail message from the law firm.

"It's because of my computer science project," I said, trying to hide behind schoolwork.

"How can a school project get a law firm representing an international company to send you a letter threatening legal action?"

"Well, you remember I mentioned that documentary I saw about how bad fast food was for you?"

My father nodded.

"This is disgusting!"

I turned around. My mother was standing at the door, peering into the room.

"This is unbelievable!" she said.

"We have bigger problems than his room," my father said. "Come in and sit down."

"Sit down? There's no place to sit! I'm afraid I could catch something—"

"Then stand up, but have a look at this. The law firm of Smith and Evans has sent our son a letter."

"They've what?" she said as she sloshed her way across my room.

"They've sent Ian an e-mail. Look."

Eric Walters

My mother stood behind where my father and I sat and looked at the screen. She leaned in and started to read.

"Scroll down," she said.

I scrolled the letter down.

"This is your basic cease-and-desist letter. What exactly did you do?"

"Nothing really." I explained about the documentary and how I came up with the idea of the boycott and spreading it through MSN and the Internet.

"And this is actually working?" my father asked.

"I don't know about the boycott, but I've had close to eight hundred e-mails since I sent it out last night."

"Unbelievable," my mother said.

"It must be believable enough that Frankie's is concerned enough to send this letter."

"But are they serious, are they really going to sue me?"

She shook her head. "I don't think so." She looked at my father. "What do you think, dear?"

"I agree. This is just a letter to threaten you. Just to be sure, show us what you sent."

I grabbed the mouse and clicked on my Sent box. I scrolled down and found the letter, double-clicking to open it. My parents read the message.

"There is nothing here that constitutes libel," my father said.

"Not that I can see," my mother agreed.

"We're allowed freedom of assembly, so I don't see how you can't be allowed freedom to not assemble. You can decide not to go to a place if you want to, and you can suggest to other people that they don't go there either."

"I agree," my mother said. "You didn't make any threats or promises or say they were frying cats or rats or serving people poison. Nothing that is a basis for a lawsuit."

"So they're not going to sue me?" I asked hopefully.

"Probably not," my mother said.

"Probably?" I questioned.

"You never can tell," my father said, "but personally, I'd love it if they tried."

"So would I!" my mother exclaimed.

"You two want me to be sued?"

"Definitely. Can you imagine the headlines? Giant multinational con-glomerate sues fifteen-year-old boy… we'd kill them!" my father said.

"After we got through counter-suing them, we'd own a big chunk of Frankie's," my mother said.

"But I'm sure it's not going to come to that," my father said. "Just to be sure, I'm going to make a phone call tomorrow to Smith and Evans. I'll let them know we'd welcome a court battle. That should be enough to make them think twice."

"Thanks...thanks a lot," I said.

"That's what parents do for their kids," my father said.

"And now you can do something for us," my mother said.

"What? Anything," I said.

My mother smiled and then motioned around the room.

"Couldn't I just get sued instead?"

Chapter Ten

I stuck a finger down the collar of
my shirt and gave a little tug. The
shirt was stiff and itchy and too tight
around the neck. I didn't know how
anybody could wear a shirt and tie to
work every day.

Oswald looked equally uncomfortable. His tie and jacket didn't
match and were too big. It looked like

he'd borrowed them from his father. Julia looked relaxed—a bit distant, but relaxed. At first I thought she was mad at me because I'd dragged her and Oswald into the meeting with the lawyers. Then I found out that wasn't it. She thought coming to this meeting, the whole idea of being threatened by a law firm, was actually quite cool. What was happening was that she and Oswald had had another "misunderstanding." That was Julia-speak, which meant she wanted Oswald to do something or say something or think something or be something, and he'd objected. Good for Oswald.

I would have liked to be someplace else, almost any place other than in the law office of Smith and Evans. Thank goodness my parents were here to "represent" me. Julia and Oswald had come along to "back me up" since they were involved too.

My mother and father, dressed in suits, sat opposite us in the waiting room. If the fanciness of this waiting room meant anything, then this firm had a lot of money, and a lot of money meant they were probably pretty good lawyers, and that meant—I stopped myself from letting my mind run off, screaming and sweating and panicking. There was no reason to panic.

"You look nervous," Julia said to me.

"I am a little. You?"

She shook her head. "It's not me they were threatening to sue."

"They're not going to sue anybody," my mother said.

"It's just a meeting," my father added. "And to be quite honest, I'm far more curious than I am worried." He looked at his watch. "They've kept us waiting almost ten minutes. The meeting was to start five minutes ago. They have five more minutes before we tell them we're leaving."

"We're going to leave?" I gasped.

"We might," he said.

"But we might not," my mother said. "It's all part of game playing."

"Like sending a threatening letter on the e-mail," my father said.

Just then the door to the inner office opened and we all turned.

"Eric, Anita, how good to see you!" a man exclaimed as he crossed the waiting room and shook hands with my parents.

"I'm surprised you're so happy to see us after we beat you so badly in court the last time we met," my father said.

"Court is court. Hopefully this is a less combative situation."

My mother introduced us to the man—Mr. Evans—one of the partners in the firm. He was friendly—almost too friendly. That made me even more nervous. He led us into a big elegant boardroom. We all took seats around the polished wooden table.

"I must admit I'm a little disappointed to hear that," my father said.

"How so?" Mr. Evans asked.

"I was really looking forward to a court battle. Can you imagine how this would play out?"

My mother laughed. "It would have been beautiful: Frankie's versus three teenagers. The very people they are trying to appeal to. The press would have eaten it up. Even if we'd lost the court battle—"

"And there's no way we would have lost," my father interjected.

"—this would have generated enough publicity to really make the boycott work," my mother finished.

"It would not have been pleasant," Mr. Evans said. "I had hoped my vague threat of legal action would have made this all go away."

"And it might have, if it wasn't aimed at somebody who has two trial lawyers as parents," my mother said.

"Yes, that was unfortunate," Mr. Evans said. "Just out of curiosity, whose idea was this boycott to begin with?"

"It was sort of all—"

"It was all Ian's idea," Oswald said, cutting me off.

Way to stand behind me—while holding a knife.

"My congratulations!" Mr. Evans beamed. "It was nothing short of brilliant!"

"Um…thank you," I mumbled.

"That e-mail you wrote was perfect. It stated your case without saying anything that was a lie. You didn't say anything like the food was poisonous."

"Then you agree that Frankie's food is bad for you?" Julia said.

"I agree it's not health food, and consuming mass amounts of it isn't a good idea. Denying that would be like denying the sky was blue, which I'd never do...unless I was hired to prove it was green."

"Or at least a greenish shade of blue," my father said. The three lawyers laughed.

Lawyers—pay them and they'll argue for, or against, anything. And my parents wondered why I didn't want to be a lawyer.

"Now, you didn't invite us all the way down here to simply offer compliments," my father said.

"No. I invited you here to make an offer."

"What sort of offer?" my mother questioned.

My parents had already explained to me—to all three of us—that asking for something from Frankie's might be seen as blackmailing them. The legal term was extortion, and you could get arrested for that. Would it be different if they offered me something without us asking?

"My client is prepared to offer lunch," Mr. Evans said.

"Lunch...but it's only nine o'clock," Julia said.

"Not lunch today and not just for the five of you," Mr. Evans said. He paused, that sort of long pause lawyers use for dramatic effect. Why didn't he just go on and spit it out?

"Frankie's will provide lunch for every single person in your entire high school...on Friday the 13th."

"That's the day of the boycott," Julia said.

"What better way to show everybody that Frankie's food is not only *fast* food, but *fine* food."

"That is brilliant," my father said admiringly.

"No it isn't!" Julia snapped. "That is so slimy!"

"Oh, it's both," my father said. "Brilliant and slimy. Is this your idea?" he asked Mr. Evans.

"I'm afraid I can't take all the credit. Of course there is one catch," Mr. Evans continued.

"There's always a catch," my mother said. "Go on."

"In response to our generous offer, we are asking that your son send an e-mail explaining what is going to happen. He must also ask everybody to send out e-mails the same way they did about the boycott."

"So let me get this straight," I said. "If I just send out an e-mail, you'll give lunch to fifteen hundred kids at my school?"

"That is correct."

"And if I don't?"

"Then I'm afraid we can't provide the lunch," Mr. Evans said. "We can't look like we're trying to undercut your efforts to boycott us. That would be unethical."

"But you are trying to undercut and you are being unethical!" Julia said. "You're trying to bribe us!"

"Bribe is such an awful word," Mr. Evans said. "I'm just trying to help you form an opinion."

"Look," I said, "even if I wanted to, what makes you think I could stop the boycott?"

"Yeah, it's like he lit a match, but now it's a gigantic forest fire. Do you really think he can stop it just by sending another e-mail?" Julia asked.

"Maybe. Maybe not. All we want is for you to try. And I guess I should also mention one other fact. As we speak there are representatives of Frankie's meeting with your principal, vice-principal and student council to put this same offer of a free lunch before them."

"So part of the reason for *this* meeting was to get us here instead of at the school," my father said.

Mr. Evans didn't answer.

"So, do we have a deal?" Mr. Evans asked.

"Unbelievable," I muttered under my breath.

"I don't understand," Mr. Evans said.

"The whole thing is unbelievable. First you try to threaten me. Then you try to bribe me. And now you do the two together, trying to bribe me and threatening me if I don't take the bribe."

"I don't like to think of it in those terms," he said.

"That's because you're a lawyer," I said.

"So are you turning down the offer?" Mr. Evans asked.

I looked at my parents for advice.

"Sorry, Ian," my mother said, "but this is up to you. You started things and you have to decide how to finish them."

"Well?" Mr. Evans asked.

"Well, I'm not going to answer...not yet...I have to consider what to do."

"Take all the time you want," Mr. Evans said. "The deal is on the table until close of business in two days."

Chapter Eleven

"Ian!"

I heard my name being called out but didn't stop or turn around. If I ignored whoever it was, maybe they'd go away.

I'd spent the whole morning with people coming up to me and thanking me for the free Frankie's lunch that was coming because of me. Or they were telling me they were "with me" in supporting the boycott and they were upset Frankie's was trying to bribe us with a burger. The student council had done a pretty good job of letting everybody in the whole school know about the free lunch offer.

I kept walking, eyes forward, down the hall, putting kids and classrooms between me and whoever had been calling.

"Ian...wait up!"

I recognized the voice—it was Julia. I stopped and spun around. She was running down the hall, a big smile on her face. She had a nice smile. It made me smile back.

"Are you going deaf?" she asked.

"Selective hearing."

"What does that mean?" she asked.

"I was trying to ignore you."

"You were trying to ignore me?" she asked, sounding hurt.

"Not *you*. I didn't know it was you calling, and when I did, I stopped.

It's everybody else in the school I'm trying to ignore…if they'd let me."

"Lots of people been bugging you, huh?"

"Everybody in the whole school," I said.

"You're always exaggerating," Julia said.

"The only one who is exaggerating is you when you say I *always* exaggerate. It certainly feels like it's everybody."

"Way to go, Ian!" a boy said as he passed by and slapped me on the back.

"Thanks."

"Who was that?" Julia asked as the boy walked away.

"I have no idea."

"At least he is on your side," Julia said.

"On my side in what way?"

"You know, supporting the boycott."

"Not necessarily," I said. "He may have been thanking me because he's getting a free lunch from Frankie's."

"You have to be kidding," she said.

I shook my head. "Nope. It's running about fifty-fifty. Half the school is backing me in the boycott and the other half is happy to be getting a free Frankie's lunch."

"How stupid. Do those people really think you'd cave in for a bunch of burgers?"

"Actually, I think a thousand burgers with fries and drinks is more than a bunch."

"It doesn't matter if it was a million burgers because I know you wouldn't trade your principles. I'm proud of you!" she said.

"You are?"

"Of course I am. Most people would have just given in, but not you."

"Thanks." I didn't have the guts to tell her I still hadn't completely made up my mind what I was going to do. Somehow, though, her words had an impact. I did want to make her proud of me.

"I was explaining to Oswald—"

"Where is Oswald?" I asked.

"Who knows…and who cares."

I gave her a questioning look. "Did you two have another misunderstanding?"

"I really don't want to talk about it. I better get to class," Julia said.

"Me too. See you later."

Julia rushed off in one direction and I hurried off in the other. I'd gone no more than a couple of dozen steps when there was a hand on my shoulder.

"Hey, buddy!"

It was Oswald. "You just missed Julia," I said.

"I know…I saw her."

"You did?"

"Yeah. I saw the two of you talking. I just waited until she left," Oswald said.

"Why did you do that?"

He shrugged. "I just feel like I need a little space. She can be a little annoying sometimes."

"A little?" I questioned.

Oswald laughed. "If I tell you something will you promise not to tell me 'I told you so'?"

"Sorry, can't make that promise."

"Okay, either way. It's just that I was thinking that maybe it wasn't such a good idea for me and Julia to start dating."

"Do you think?"

"Okay, okay, I know you told me, and I know I should have listened to you, but what's done is done."

"So are you going to break up with her?" I asked.

"I would, but I'm sort of afraid of her."

This time I did laugh.

"Glad you think this is funny!"

"Well, it *is* funny. What do you think she'd do, beat you up?" I asked.

"No…probably not. It just would be easier if she broke up with me."

"I have an idea how you could do that."

"You do?"

"Yeah. Just tell her you think I should try to cancel the boycott and get burgers for everybody."

"Do you think that would work?"

"She's pretty clear about wanting the boycott."

"Then, sure, I could tell her that." He paused. "Do you think *you* could tell her that for me?"

"You really are afraid. Sorry, but I'm not doing your dirty work."

"I guess that's fair. Besides, that wouldn't even be a lie about the boycott," Oswald said.

"It wouldn't?"

"If it was me, I'd just write another e-mail. I don't think there's anything wrong with us all getting a free lunch."

"If that's what you believe, Oswald, then that's what you should tell her. Just be careful. She might actually take a swing at you."

"I could live with that. Thanks for the idea. See you later."

"Yeah, later."

At that instant the bell rang. I was officially late for class. If you got there just after the bell, most teachers would still let you in. Unfortunately this wasn't most teachers—I was now late for law and Mr. Phillips, the teacher who had gotten me suspended. And he had the stupidest rule in the world. If the bell had gone and his door was closed, you had to "make a plea." You had to claim you were "guilty" of being late and be sent down to the office for a late slip, or argue that it truly wasn't your fault and you "weren't guilty," and he, as the "judge," decided whether to admit you or send you down to the office. Talk about stupid.

I turned the corner of the hall just in time to see the door to his classroom close. That settled it. I had a pretty good excuse, but I wasn't going to play his game. I'd just go down and get a late slip.

"Hey, I-Man!" a voice yelled behind me.

I turned. There were five guys walking toward me. I knew them. Everybody knew them. They were the core group of a bunch of losers—kids who were making high school into a career rather than a four-year project. Maybe they figured if they hung around long enough the school would either give them a mercy pass or they'd become so old they would automatically become teachers.

They shuffled down the hall, and the few kids still around got out of their way. They stopped directly in front of me—well, sort of in front and beside, and one kid shifted over so he was behind me as well. I was surrounded. I felt uneasy and a bit scared.

"So, we heard you're the one who's getting us all a free lunch," Tony, the biggest of the big guys, said.

"Um, yeah, I guess, maybe."

"Maybe? What does that mean?" he asked.

"It's just that I haven't really made up my mind what I'm going to do," I said sheepishly.

They all looked confused.

"It's just that they're only going to give everybody the lunch if I agree to go online and tell people not to support the boycott," I explained.

"That makes sense. You couldn't really ask people to support a boycott when everybody in the school is eating their food."

"So you understand!" I said hopefully.

"I understand good. I understand that if I don't eat I get a little cranky, and when I get cranky there ain't no telling what might happen."

Tony suddenly reached out, grabbed me by the front of the shirt and slammed me into the lockers. He crowded into me. His friends all moved in closer too.

"Nobody cheats me out of a free meal!" Tony snarled.

"I...I could buy you a lunch," I stammered.

Tony let go of my shirt but didn't move. He smiled. No, it wasn't a smile, it was a smirk.

"You must be one rich kid," Tony said.

"It's under five bucks for a burger combo."

"Yeah, but that's five bucks times twenty of us. You think I'm gonna eat without my buddies? You gonna feed all of us? You got two hundred bucks?"

"A hundred dollars," I said, doing the math in my head.

"A hundred, two hundred, it don't matter to me 'cause I'm not the one buying the lunches. And believe me, we better be getting lunch that day or somebody is going to get a serious bellyache."

He balled his hand into a fist, holding it inches from my face. This was unbelievable. Right here, right now, I was going to get beaten up!

"Hey!"

We all turned. It was Mr. Phillips. His door was open and he was walking toward us. I never thought I'd be happy to see him.

"All of you get to class. Now!"

Tony didn't move. He looked at Mr. Phillips and then he looked at me. Then he smiled.

"We'll be seeing each other later...for lunch. Be sure to bring your wallet."

Tony and his buddies slowly sauntered down the hall as Mr. Phillips approached. I stood there, still shaking, too stunned to move.

"You okay?" he asked.

I nodded.

"Is this another example of your sparkling personality making friends and influencing people?" he asked.

"I didn't do anything!" I protested.

"Then it has to do with this whole Frankie's thing, I would imagine."

"It does!" I said.

He slowly shook his head. "Those people are geniuses."

"What do you mean?" I asked defensively.

"You do something that's perfectly legal to make life difficult for them, and they figure out something, again perfectly legal, to make your life difficult."

"To make my life impossible," I said.

"We just started talking about the situation in class—the class you're late for—when I noticed you weren't there, and somebody said they just saw you in the hall."

"It wasn't my fault."

"I believe it. Your boycott has been the subject of my class all day. It's amazing how it's divided the school. No matter what you do, what you decide, half the school is going to be mad at you."

"You got that right. Either way I'm wrong. Either way I can't win."

"Maybe the lesson here is that if you fight with the big boys you better be prepared to get hit by the big boys. You must wish you'd never started this," he said.

"You got that right."

Mr. Phillips looked at me. "What if I was able to show you a way out of this? A way where you can't lose."

"That's impossible," I scoffed.

"Do you want to hear my idea or not?"

I didn't answer right away.

"Well?"

"I want to hear your idea," I said.

Chapter Twelve

I peeked around the stage curtains and watched as the whole school slowly filed into the auditorium. I tried to pick out the familiar faces of Julia and Oswald, but I couldn't see them. I couldn't see my parents either. I knew my friends would be there, but there was a good chance my parents wouldn't. They had a

Eric Walters

pre-trial hearing and probably wouldn't
be through in time.

"Good afternoon, Ian."

I jumped, startled from my thoughts.
It was Mr. Evans. He had a smile on
his face and extended his hand to shake
mine.

"It was very nice of your school to
invite me to be here today," he said. "Do
I have you to thank?"

"Not me. Mr. Phillips...my law
teacher."

"I'll have to offer my thanks," he said.
"As a spokesperson for Frankie's, all we
could ever ask for is the opportunity to
present our message."

What he meant was he was glad he
had a chance to brainwash people.

"I see that there will be just the two
of us speaking," Mr. Evans said as he
held up the program. "Me, and then
you. Do you know what you're going
to say?"

"I have a rough idea," I said. What I didn't let on was that I'd been up most of the night writing and rehearsing my speech.

"Do you want to run it by me? Maybe I can help you, offer suggestions perhaps."

"That's okay. I think it's better if it just comes from me."

He figured we'd invited him here to formally announce the free lunch and that I was calling off the boycott. That's what he thought, but not knowing for sure was bothering him.

"They say you should always save the best speaker for last," Mr. Evans said. "So your speech has to be awfully good."

I knew what he was doing. He was trying to bother me, make me nervous. I was already nervous, but his trying to make me more nervous was having the opposite effect. Instead of nervous I was getting angry.

"I've heard that most people hate public speaking," Mr. Evans continued. "How about you?"

"I've heard that too."

"I meant, how do *you* feel about standing up in front of an audience and talking? Does it make you nervous?"

"What's to be nervous about?" I asked, trying to sound calm and cool— exactly what I wasn't feeling inside.

"For starters, you're appearing before everybody in your whole school, and every single person is listening to you… the kids you go to school with every day…strangers…your teachers…your best friends…maybe that girl you have a crush on."

Julia's image popped into my mind. But that was because she was a close friend, not because I had a crush on her.

"And if you make a single mistake, a little mistake, that's all they'll hear, all they'll remember and talk about for days, maybe even weeks after," he continued.

What a jerk. What a big, mean, stupid jerk!

"I never thought of it that way," I said, trying to hide both my nerves and my anger. "I thought it would be *you* who should be nervous."

"Me?" he scoffed.

"Yeah. I'm just a kid," I said with a shrug. "If I say something stupid, nobody will be surprised. I'm almost *supposed* to screw up…but you…that's different. If you aren't perfect—heck, even if you *are* perfect and the boycott happens anyway—then Frankie's will be mad at you. They might just fire you and your firm! Maybe my parents' law firm can put in an offer to take over from you."

He didn't say a word. His only answer was a reddening face. He didn't look friendly. He looked annoyed, even a little bit angry. I looked out through the curtains.

"Can we have everybody take their seats?" Mr. Phillips announced as he stood at the podium. "We'd like to begin."

The noise in the auditorium started to die down. Soon there was silence.

"We have assembled today, as the student body, to hear a special proposal," Mr. Phillips said. "Here to explain the details of this proposal is Mr. David Evans, a senior partner in the law firm that represents Frankie's restaurants. Please welcome our guest."

The audience began clapping and Mr. Evans walked across the stage. He shook hands with Mr. Phillips and then leaned forward and said something into his ear—probably thanking him as he'd said he was going to do. He then settled in behind the podium, adjusted the microphone and waited for silence before beginning.

"What a pleasure it is for me to be here today," he said. "I know there are many students in the audience who are members of the Frankie's family, who are amongst the *123,000* employees we have worldwide!"

Mr. Evans was right. I knew seven kids who worked at Frankie's, and I only knew a quarter of the kids in the school.

"These associates are not only given opportunities to develop work skills and earn money, but are also eligible for university scholarships. Each year Frankie's helps to send hundreds of students to university and college. This is just one of the many things we do for our community," Mr. Evans continued.

"We are an industry leader in recycling of plastics and cardboard. We support charities and local sports teams.

We are a good corporate citizen." He seemed to be hitting his stride.

"Now, sometimes a company as big as ours can be accused of making mistakes. Is there anybody here who hasn't been accused of doing something wrong?" he asked, and then he paused.

"One of your fellow students, a wonderful young man who is to speak after me, started an e-mail chain letter designed to create a one-day boycott. Not that we want that to happen, but we applaud his imagination and efforts. All he was trying to do was make a difference—just like the people at Frankie's are trying to make a difference.

"We at Frankie's are on your side. We care about you and we care about what you think about us. And because of that we've made an offer. Let me restate it. Next week, on Friday the 13th, we'd like to bring to your school a complete

Frankie's lunch for each student and staff member! And remember, Frankie's is more than fast food...Frankie's is your friend!"

The audience erupted in cheers and screams and applause. There wasn't much question how people felt. Maybe there was no point in me even talking. Maybe I should just go up, thank Mr. Evans and be done with it.

"Thank you all!" Mr. Evans said. He shook hands with Mr. Phillips and walked offstage as the audience continued to clap.

He smiled at me. "You heard how they reacted," he said. "I don't think *I* have anything to worry about. Go ahead, tell them you're going to call off the boycott...make everybody happy." He paused. "And don't be nervous."

Chapter Thirteen

In an instant I went from nervous to angry. He was enjoying this, enjoying beating me, stopping the boycott and defending his precious client. I had to fight the urge to reach out and slap that smug little smile off his face.

"And now," Mr. Phillips announced, "could we please welcome one of our own, one of my best students, Ian Cheevers!"

The crowd started cheering and my knees got weak. I was frozen in place.

"You better get going," Mr. Evans said.

His words unstuck me. I started across the stage. The lights were bright and for a split second I was blinded. I focused on Mr. Phillips. He offered his hand and we shook as people kept on clapping. I thought I heard Julia yell out my name.

"Just say what you're going to say," Mr. Phillips said in my ear. "And remember, you *can't* lose."

I looked up at him. He was right. I couldn't lose.

I stood in front of the podium and looked out at the audience. I focused on the first few rows, filled with kids and teachers, people I knew, people

I recognized and people who were complete strangers. The clapping had stopped. The whole room was silent, waiting for me to begin.

I leaned into the microphone. "Hello," I began, my voice cracking over the word. I took a deep breath. "I just wanted to start by saying...by saying that you're all *stupid*. You're all a bunch of *stupid losers* who can be easily tricked and fooled."

There was stunned silence and then people began booing! I stepped back from the microphone and the booing continued.

Mr. Phillips walked back up to the podium and raised his hands to silence the crowd. "Please, allow our speaker to continue."

It got silent again, but this time it was an angry silence.

"Go on," Mr. Phillips said to me quietly.

"It isn't *me* who thinks you're stupid and it isn't me who thinks you're all losers. It's Frankie's and it's Mr. Evans. Actually, they think I'm a stupid loser too. They think we're all stupid. How do I know that? They say they're leaders in recycling, but we all know that a major source of garbage on the streets and in landfills is Frankie's. They say they care for you, but instead of feeding you good food they serve the unhealthiest food in the industry. They say they care for the people who work for them, but they give them no benefits and pay minimum wages. Why do they do that? Because all they really care about is money. They can make more money selling soda than they can selling orange juice. They can make more money selling burgers and fries than they can selling salads and fruits. They care about themselves, about the money they make." I took a breath.

"For years they've been tricking you into eating at their restaurants. They've been offering you plastic toys and contests and play places to get you in and eating their food. And today they want to trick you again." I paused. "Maybe trick isn't the right word. *Bribe* is better. They figure because we're a bunch of teenagers we don't have any brains or integrity. They figure that if they offer us a Frankie's lunch we'll do what they want us to do and not what we should do. They figure we think with our stomachs and not with our brains.

"Next Friday I'm not going to eat at Frankie's. That's my choice. But I'm not here to make *your* choice. I'm not here to try to trick you or make your decision for you. That's up to you. I'm here to let you have the power to make the decision. You've heard Mr. Evans speak and you've heard me speak. Now it's up to you."

Mr. Phillips walked back up to the podium.

"Could we please turn up the house lights," he said.

The auditorium became visible as row after row of the ceiling lights came to life. I scanned the crowd. I saw lots of people I knew—my entire computer science class was sitting together, and the principal was standing beside them, and there were Julia and Oswald sitting together! Julia waved her arms at me and I waved back. She flashed me a big smile. She looked so happy. Was that because she and Oswald had resolved their latest fight or because of what I'd said…was she proud of me?

My goodness, here I was standing in front of the whole school, doing probably the most important thing in my whole life, and I was thinking about what Julia was thinking. Maybe I *did* have a crush on her.

"Today," Mr. Phillips began, "you are being given a unique opportunity. You are bright, well-informed young adults. Today you will be the judges, or more correctly, the jury. You are going to vote. You have two choices. You can either support the boycott or vote for the free Frankie's lunch. Simple rules. One person, one vote. The majority rules. If you vote for the lunch, then Ian has agreed to try to cancel the boycott."

I nodded my head.

"Here's how you will vote. When I ask if you support the boycott you will rise to your feet and stand. If you want the meal you will remain seated." He turned to me. "Anything else, Ian?"

"Nothing."

"Okay, on the count of three we want you to either stand or stay seated. One…"

I felt my whole body tingle.

"Two…"

I took a deep breath.

"Three!"

Julia practically jumped to her feet, as did dozens and dozens of other people. Then a whole row, and pockets and patches around the whole room stood up. I quickly tried to estimate…were there more people standing or sitting down? As I tried to figure it out, more and more and more people got to their feet, and then a bunch of them started to climb up onto their seats, cheering and whistling and clapping. The noise was deafening. I looked around the entire room…more and more and more people rose until there wasn't a single person sitting down!

Mr. Evans moved onto the stage and stood beside me. "You really are your parents' child," he yelled into my ear.

"I take that as a compliment."

"That's how it was meant. I assume you're going to become a lawyer when you grow up."

"Who knows?" I said and shrugged. It had been a buzz up there presenting my case.

"When you become a lawyer, you come and see me and you got yourself a job!"

"Thanks, but I think I'll be working for another firm."

"Come and see me. I'll top the offer your parents make."

Chapter Fourteen

I held the phone to my ear. Elevator music played while I was on hold. At the far end of the room, my parents sat staring at the TV. It was tuned to *Good Morning New York!*

"Are you there, Ian?" a voice asked.

"I'm here."

"Good. You're up next."

"I'll stay right here," I said.

"And now, on the phone," the TV host said, "we have a young man who has created quite a controversy. He's fifteen and he lives in New York. His name is Ian Cheevers. For those who haven't heard, he is the young man who started a boycott of Frankie's Fast Foods. Are you there, Ian?"

His voice was suddenly coming from the phone. It startled me. "Yes...yes, I'm here."

"Now we all know that you started the boycott after watching the movie *Stuffed*. What gave you the idea to use the Internet?"

"It was part of a school project on mass communication," I said. "The idea popped into my head and I talked it over with my friends Julia and Oswald."

"And they were in favor?" he asked.

"They thought it was great."

"So it started with you e-mailing forty people and asking them to each e-mail another forty people who e-mailed forty people."

"That's how it started and it just grew, getting forty times bigger each time people sent out their messages," I explained.

"How do you feel about the results?" he asked.

"What do you mean?" I asked.

"Our reports indicate that business at Frankie's nationwide was down almost forty percent, while in certain areas, like New York and Los Angeles, it dropped by almost sixty percent today."

"Wow," I muttered.

"Wow is right," the host laughed.

"But I didn't do it to drive down their business," I said. "I did it to send them a message that they have to change their menu to promote more healthy eating."

"And do you think they got the message?" he asked.

"I don't know," I said. "What I do know is that we can do this again next Friday, and the Friday after that and the Friday after that."

"That sounds like a threat," he said.

"No, not a threat. A promise."

The man laughed again. "Just out of curiosity, what do you think of our show?"

"I like it."

"That's good. I wouldn't want you mad at us. Thanks for being with us, Ian."

"Thanks," I said.

The line went dead. I hung up.

"And in a related story," the TV host said, "Frankie's Fast Foods has called a press conference for tomorrow. I have it from reliable sources that they will be announcing a revised menu which will include healthy choices."

"Congratulations, Ian, perhaps you did get the results you wanted," said my dad.

"Not just me," I said. "I just started it."

"Every idea in history started with one person. Congrat—"

The phone rang. I picked it up.

"Way to go, Ian!" It was Julia.

"It went okay," I said, trying to practice sounding modest.

"Don't be a jerk. You must be thrilled."

"You're telling *me* how I'm supposed to feel now?" I demanded.

"Well, I can't tell Oswald anymore."

The two of them had formally broken up the week before. It was like a mercy killing.

"You want to go to a movie tonight?" Julia asked.

"Yeah, sure. What do you want to see?" I asked.

"You decide."

"Me? Maybe the three of us should talk it over. Want me to call Oswald?"

There was silence. "Not really. It's still pretty uncomfortable for me and him. I was thinking it could just be the two of us."

"You asking me out on a date?"

"Don't flatter yourself!" she snapped. "So you want to go or not?"

"I guess." I paused. "Just out of curiosity, if *I* did, you know, ask you out, what would you say?"

"Depends," she said.

"Depends on what?"

"On what you were asking me to do. For example, if you were inviting me out to go to a movie, I might just say yes."

I took a deep breath and felt my heart pounding. I could do this. "Julia, do you think that tonight, me and you, do you think we could maybe go out together to see a movie?"

The phone was silent. "A movie...that would be nice."